This book is dedicated to my young readers and
You are my inspiration

Thank you for choosing my book.

As a sign of my appreciation, please get your free ebook:

Scan the QR code below to get your free book

ISBN 978-0-473-58738-3 (paperback)
ISBN 978-0-473-58739-0 (epub)

www.adrianlaurent.com

Calm Anger

By Adrian Laurent

This Book Belongs To:

_____

One day after school, Ella wanted to watch TV.
"Not yet," Mom said. "It's not watching time, sweetie."

Ella felt mad. Her face turned bright red.
She wanted to shout, but Ella waited instead.

She calmed herself down by counting to ten.
When she felt better, she asked Mom again.

"No," Mom repeated, and Ella huffed.
"I see you're frustrated," Mom said. "Waiting is tough."

Again Ella felt angry, her temper built to a rage.
She wanted to open a book and rip out a page.

She wanted to stomp and make the house shake.
Ella had big feelings, but knew she shouldn't break.

Ella waited, and breathed, then asked Mom again.
"It's not watching time yet," Mom gently explained.

"Perhaps go outside and take a walk instead."
"You'll burn off your anger with exercise," Mom said.

Ella didn't want to walk. That would take too long.
So she turned on her music and played her best song.

Then she went to her room and ran in one spot.
The more puffed she was, the less angry she got.

"Good job, Ella," Mom said. "You tried hard to calm down."
"I have an idea to help turn things around."

"Is it watching time yet?" Ella asked once again.
Mom shook her head. "Ella, I will tell you when."

"Let's do something together, it will be fun."
Ella's face lit up in a smile as bright as the sun.
Mom walked to the garage and pulled out a box.
"Now take off your shoes," Mom said. "Not your socks."

Mom found things to craft with then set them down.
The mood in the house had turned around.
Ella wasn't sure what was happening yet.
But she was going to enjoy it, she'd safely bet.

First, they drew a door, complete with a knob,
Then painted a window, brushing glob by glob.
They drew on some siding. Brick by brick they went.
They drew until their fingers hurt and they were spent.

Then they folded the box and made a house.
Ella climbed in to play like she was a mouse.
"Ok Ella, it's watching time now," Mom said.
But Ella crawled out and shook her head.

"No thanks, Mom," Ella said. "I'm fine in my box,"
"I couldn't watch TV before, but thanks a lot!"
"If I had, I wouldn't have this house for play."
"But now I do and can watch TV another day."

The End

Download a PDF of all the illustrations in black and white to use as coloring pages.

Scan the QR code below to get your free book

Thank you for reading my book.

As a sign of my appreciation, please get your free ebook.

Scan the QR code below to get your free book:

I hope you enjoyed the story.

Reviews from fantastic readers like you help other parents find this book and give them confidence to choose it.

I would be so grateful if you could take one minute to leave your honest feedback about the book.

Thank you!

Adrian Laurent
Children's Book Author